W9-AYA-322

Mighty Machines
BULLDOZERS

Amanda Askew

QEB Publishing

Words in **bold** can be found
in the Glossary on page 23.

Copyright © QEB Publishing, Inc. 2010

Published in the United States by
QEB Publishing, Inc.
3 Wrigley, Suite A
Irvine, CA 92618

www.qed-publishing.co.uk

All rights reserved. No part of this publication may be reproduced,
stored in a retrieval system, or transmitted in any form or by any means,
electronic, mechanical, photocopying, recording, or otherwise, without the
prior permission of the publisher, nor be otherwise circulated in any form
of binding or cover other than that in which it is published and without a
similar condition being imposed on the subsequent purchaser.

A CIP record for this book is available from the Library of Congress.

ISBN 978 1 60992 358 7

Printed in China

Written by Amanda Askew
Designed by Phil and Traci Morash (Fineline Studios)
Editor Angela Royston
Picture Researcher Maria Joannou

Printed in China

Picture credits
Key: t = top, b = bottom, c = center, FC = front cover, BC = back cover

Alamy Images David R. Frazier Photolibrary, Inc 10l; **Getty Images**
AFP/David Furst/Stringer 14l, Jeff T. Green/Stringer 19t; **Istockphoto**
Filonmar 6–7, Ivanastar 9t, Emre Ogan 12–13, Jowita Stachowiak 18–19,
22bl; **Komatsu America** 20–21, 21t; **Photolibrary** Age Fotostock/
Dennis MacDonald 10–11, 22tl; **Shutterstock** BC, Buhanstov Alexey FC,
Dmitry Kalinovsky 1, 8–9, Ownway 4–5, 22bc, Zolwiks 5r, Jose Gil 13t,
22tr, Christina Richards 16b, Catalin Petolea 16–17, 22br; **US Air Force**
Master Sgt Rickie D. Bickle 14–15, 22tc

Contents

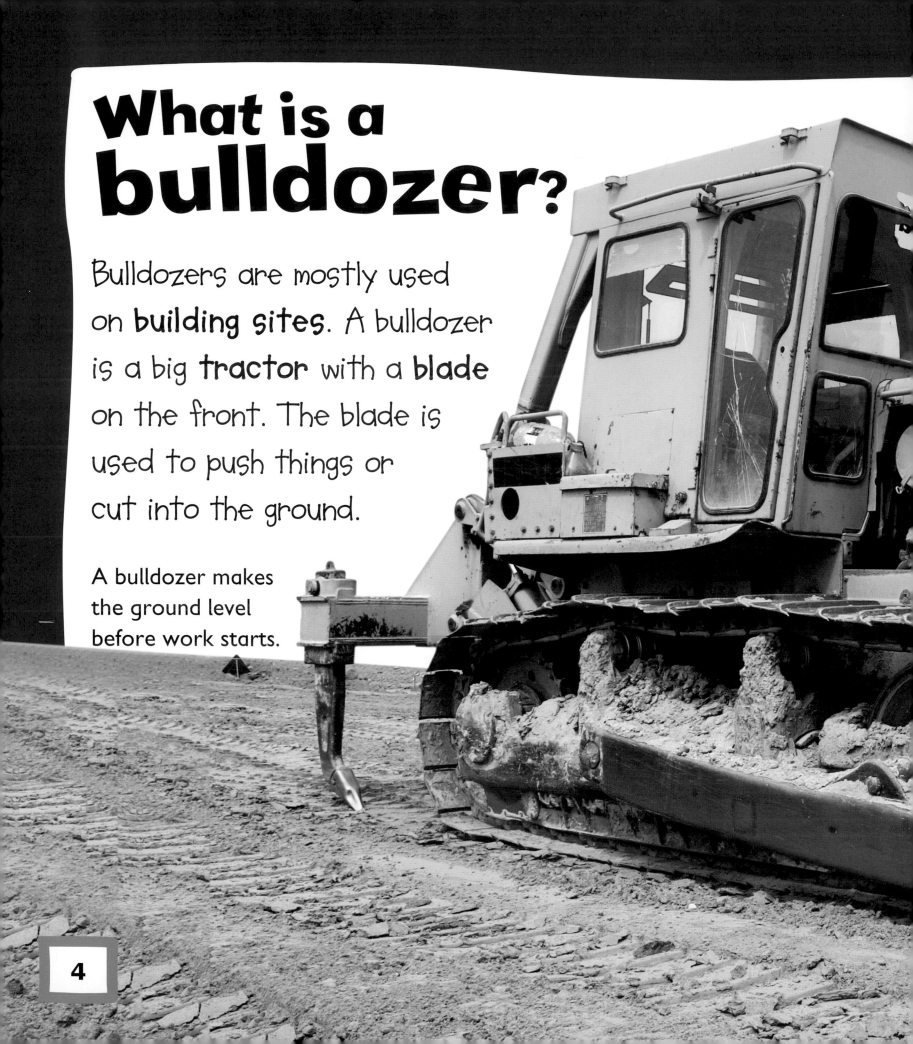

What is a bulldozer?

Bulldozers are mostly used on **building sites**. A bulldozer is a big **tractor** with a **blade** on the front. The blade is used to push things or cut into the ground.

A bulldozer makes the ground level before work starts.

A bulldozer has **tracks** instead of wheels. The tracks help the machine to move across rough ground. If a bulldozer had wheels, it would probably slip and slide.

A bulldozer has wide tracks. They stop the machine from sinking into the ground.

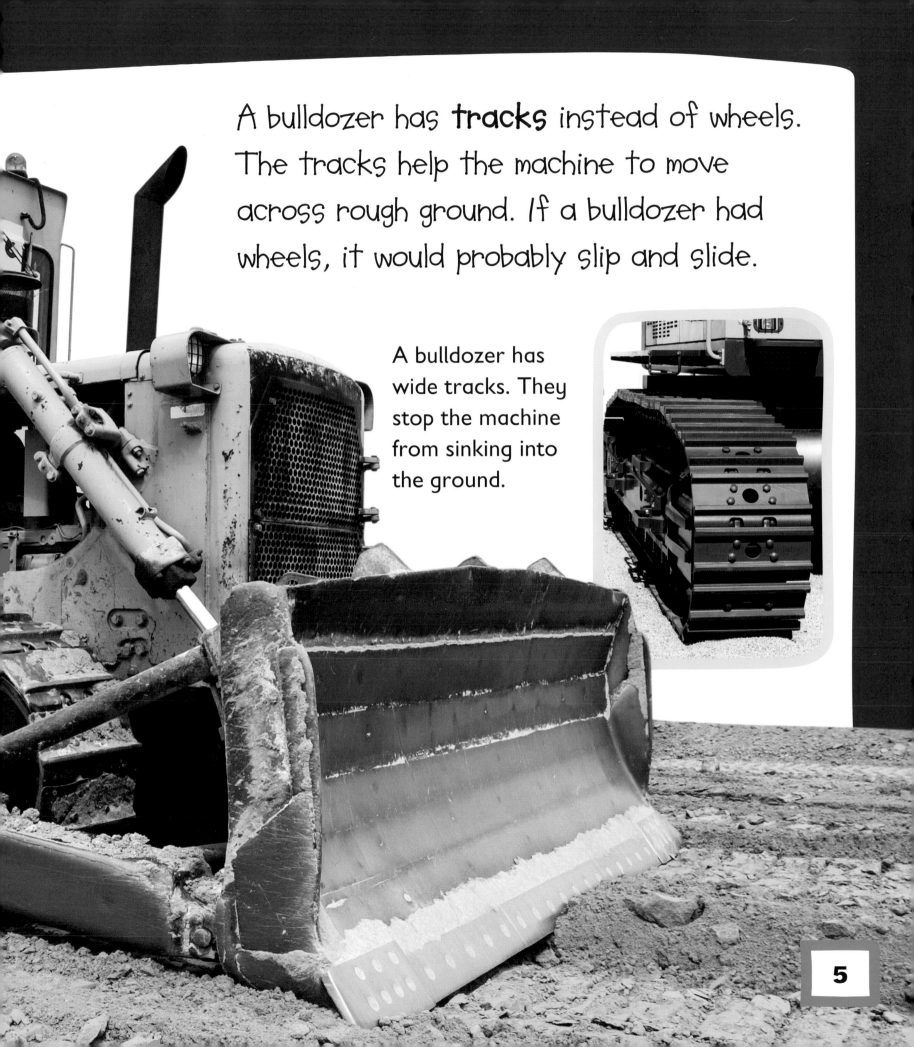

Parts of a **bulldozer**

A bulldozer has two main parts —a tractor and a blade. When the blade pushes downward, it cuts into the earth. When the blade pushes forward, it moves the pile of earth.

tractor

The tractor is the main part of the bulldozer. The driver sits in the cab and controls the machine.

blade

cab

ripper

tracks

Blades and rippers

The bulldozer uses its blade to spread out uneven earth. This makes the ground flat.

The blade is on the front of the tractor. There are many shapes and sizes of blade. Most bulldozers have a straight blade, but some have curved blades.

The **ripper** is a large claw on the back of the tractor. The ripper "rips" into the ground and breaks it up.

This ripper is about to break up the hard ground.

Building roads

Asphalt has to be laid on flat ground. A bulldozer flattens the ground so a new road can be built.

The bulldozer pushes and spreads huge mounds of earth to make the road flat.

The bulldozer goes over the same ground many times. First, it spreads the large mounds of earth, and then it evens out any small lumps or bumps.

This bulldozer is making the ground even flatter.

Mining and quarrying

Large and small bulldozers are used at **mines** and **quarries**. They clear piles of rocks. The small machines can work where there isn't much room.

Some bulldozers use a special blade, called an "SU blade". The blade is so large, it can push piles of big rocks.

This SU blade turns up at the sides. The sides hold the rocks on the blade.

This machine is moving loose rocks.

In the **army**

Soldiers use bulldozers to clear a path through thick forests or across uneven land. Sometimes, a bulldozer blade is fitted to a tank.

These bulldozers and tanks are crossing rough ground.

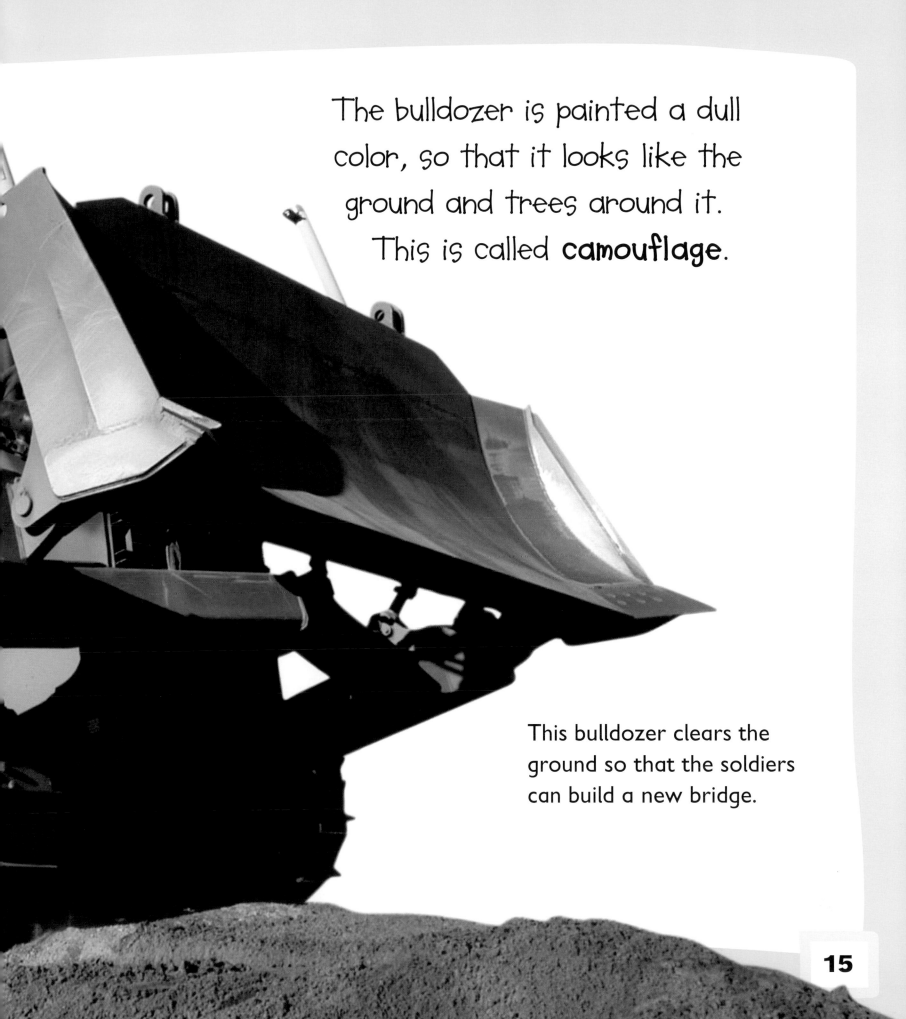

The bulldozer is painted a dull color, so that it looks like the ground and trees around it. This is called **camouflage**.

This bulldozer clears the ground so that the soldiers can build a new bridge.

On the farm

Some farmers use bulldozers to break up very hard ground. A **plow** cannot work when the ground is too hard.

The bulldozer is digging up the roots of a fallen tree.

A ripper is dragged through hard ground to break it up. The farmer can then plow the land and plant crops.

A ripper can have one spike or lots of spikes.

17

Plowing the Snow

Bulldozers make good **snowplows!** The blade clears a path through the snow or ice. The tracks stop the bulldozer from sliding on the slippery ground.

A snowplow stops cars and people from being blocked in by the snow.

A train can clear a track much faster than a bulldozer!

Trains can have a blade fitted to the front, just like a bulldozer. The blade clears snow from the railway tracks.

Biggest and smallest

The biggest bulldozer in the world is a Super Dozer. Its blade is 23 feet (7 meters) wide. Four adults could lie along it head to toe!

This monster machine can push 140 tons (127 tonnes) of rocks in one go. That's the same weight as 20 elephants!

The blade on this mini bulldozer is 28 inches (70 centimeters) wide—no wider than two and a half of these books laid end to end!

Small machines are perfect for working in small spaces.

Activities

- Here are three bulldozers from the book. Can you remember what they do?

  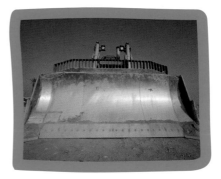

- If you needed to break up hard ground, which attachment would you use? Why did you choose that attachment?

- Draw a bulldozer building a road. Which bulldozer did you choose? What color is it? Who is driving it?

- Which picture shows a ripper?

Glossary

Asphalt
A hard material used to make the surface of roads.

Blade
A large, flat attachment used for cutting or pushing earth.

Building site
A place where a house or other building is being built.

Camouflage
A way to hide something by making it the same color as the place it is in.

Mine
A deep hole in the ground. Coal is often found in a mine.

Plow
A machine that turns over the soil to make it ready for seeds to be planted.

Quarry
A place where stone and sand are dug out of the ground.

Ripper
An attachment with a spike or spikes for breaking up hard ground.

Snowplow
A machine that is used to move snow from roads.

Tracks
A long, metal band around the wheels on a bulldozer.

Tractor
A farm machine with big wheels.

Index